D1032272

39009000056693

The Knights of
Labor and the
Haymarket Riot

DUE DATE

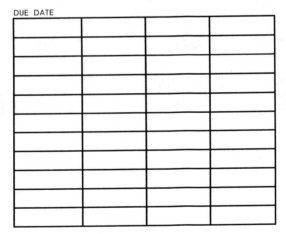

AMERICA'S INDUSTRIAL SOCIETY IN THE 19TH CENTURY ™

The Knights of Labor and the Haymarket Riot

The Fight for an Eight-Hour Workday

Bernadette Brexel

rosen central
Primary Source ™

The Rosen Publishing Group, Inc., New York

To Shima

Published in 2004 by The Rosen Publishing Group, Inc.
29 East 21st Street, New York, NY 10010

Library of Congress Cataloging-in-Publication Data

Brexel, Bernadette.
The Knights of Labor and the Haymarket Riot : the fight for an eight-hour workday/by Bernadette Brexel.—1st ed.
        p. cm.—(America's industrial society in the 19th century.)
Summary: Examines the early history of America's labor movement in the nineteenth century, particularly the fight for an eight-hour work day, and its effects on American business and workers. Includes bibliographical references and index.
ISBN 0-8239-4028-4 (library binding)
ISBN 0-8239-4283-X (paperback)
6-pack ISBN 0-8239-4295-3
1. Knights of Labor—History. 2. Haymarket Square Riot, Chicago, Ill., 1886. 3. Hours of labor—United States—History—19th century. 4. Eight-hour movement—United States—History—19th century. 5. Labor movement—United States—History—19th century. [1. Knights of Labor—History. 2. Haymarket Square Riot, Chicago, Ill., 1886. 3. Labor movement—History.]
I. Title. II. Series: America's industrial society in the nineteenth century.
HD8055.K7B67 2004b
977.3'11041—dc21

                                                                2003001255

Manufactured in the United States of America

On the cover: enlarged image: Rioters throw bomb into crowd at Haymarket Square, Chicago, 1886. First row (from left to right): steamship docked at a landing; Tammany Hall on election night, 1859; map showing U.S. railroad routes in 1883; detail of bank note, 1822, Bank of the Commonwealth of Kentucky; People's Populist Party Convention at Columbus, Nebraska, 1890; Republican ticket, 1865. Second row (from left to right): William McKinley gives a campaign speech in 1896; parade banner of the Veterans of the Haymarket Riot; Alexander Graham Bell's sketch of the telephone, c. 1876; public declaration of the government's ability to crush monopolies; City planners' illustration of Stockton, California; railroad construction camp, Nebraska, 1889.

Photo credits: cover, pp. 5, 8, 20, 24 © Library of Congress, Prints and Photographs Division; pp. 6, 17 © Hulton/Archive/Getty Images; pp. 10, 15, 27 © Bettmann/Corbis; pp. 16, 23 © Corbis; p. 26 © Library of Congress, Serial and Government Publications.

Designer: Tahara Hasan; **Editor:** Mark Beyer

Contents

1
Dangerous Labor

Some countries in the world force children to work in factories. Children are forced to work for as little as ten cents a day. They do not go to school or enjoy a regular life. They work hard to make goods. The goods are sold to make money. Child labor is against the law in the United States.

Some foreign factories hire only adults but have big workloads. Employees must complete this work in a single shift. A person's shift can be as long as twelve hours per day. These shifts are too long. Forcing employees to work this long can cause health problems. Sometimes the

Children of factory workers in the late nineteenth century also worked. Here, children are stripping leaves in a tobacco factory. Entire families had to do factory work to survive. Sometimes children worked more than ten hours each day. This left no time for education. Without education, a family could not hope to better itself.

HARPER'S
NEW MONTHLY MAGAZINE.

No. CCLXXIX.—AUGUST, 1873.—Vol. XLVII.

THE LITTLE LABORERS OF NEW YORK CITY.

LITTLE TOBACCO STRIPPERS.

ONE of the most touching facts to any one examining the lower strata of New York is the great number of young children toiling in factories and shops. With the children of the fortunate classes there are certain years of childhood which every parent feels ought to be freed from the burdens and responsibilities of life. The "struggle for existence," the labor of money-making, the toil for support, and all the cares and anxieties therewith, will come soon enough. And the parent is glad that the first years

indulge in no such sentiments. He is compelled to harness the little one very early to the car of labor, or if he be not forced to this, he is indifferent to the child's natural growth and improvement, and believes that his boy ought to pass through the same hard experience which he had himself. He is struggling with poverty, and eager for every little addition which he can make to his income. The child's wages seem to him important, and, indeed, it requires a character of more disinterestedness and a mind of factories are not safe. A factory may have dangerous machines that can harm workers.

Most of these problems do not happen in the United States. This is because we have labor laws and unions. Labor laws are made by our government. The laws tell us what is and is not allowed in the workplace. Most of these laws were made because of unions.

A union is an organization or group of workers. Unions unite a group of workers at a company. Unions

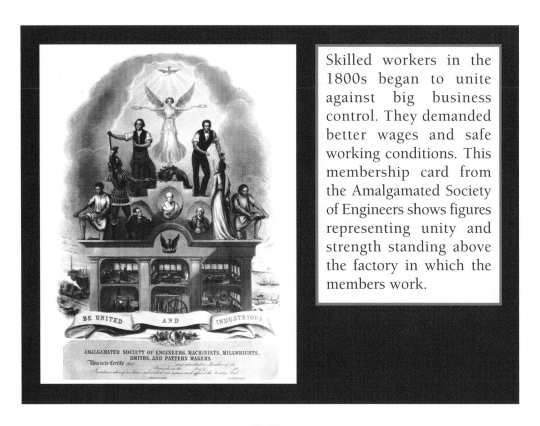

Skilled workers in the 1800s began to unite against big business control. They demanded better wages and safe working conditions. This membership card from the Amalgamated Society of Engineers shows figures representing unity and strength standing above the factory in which the members work.

Small labor unions began to join together in the late 1800s. In 1881, Samuel Gompers (above) helped found the Federation of Organized Trades and Labor Unions. Nationwide labor unions held a lot of power. They quickly gained better wages for their members.

also unite many workers across the United States. A worker who joins a union becomes a member. The union represents or speaks officially for that member. Union officials and factory officials work together. They

try to make a contract that makes both the factory and the workers happy.

Labor unions make sure that employers do not treat workers unfairly. Unions also work with politicians and government officials. Unions try to get labor laws passed.

American workers were not always treated fairly. More than one hundred years ago, child labor was common in the United States. Some shifts were longer than sixteen hours. The workers were tired and unhappy. Some workers were injured while using dangerous machines. Some machines caused unhealthy smoke. This caused breathing problems. Some jobs were very dangerous. Miners were often killed in dynamite accidents.

Early American workers formed unions to change work conditions. Unions appeared in the 1800s. Unions were part of the labor movement. The labor movement was a group of people united in the belief that work conditions could be better. Workers wanted better pay. They wanted fewer hours on the job. They wanted safer factories. They wanted a better life.

2
The Gilded Age

America became independent from England in 1783. The American people made a new government. This government protected and governed the American people. Many immigrants moved to America to become citizens.

The government had to solve problems to keep peace in America. One important problem was slavery. Northern states wanted to get rid of slavery. Southern states wanted to keep slavery. Southern plantation owners used slaves for labor. They did not have to pay their slaves. Many slaves were from Africa. Some slaves were European. All slaves were brought to America in order to work for rich landowners and businessmen. Slaves had to work as many hours as their owners wanted. Slaves were also beaten and sometimes murdered.

Slavery was an issue that was part of the Civil War in 1861. The war was fought between the Northern and

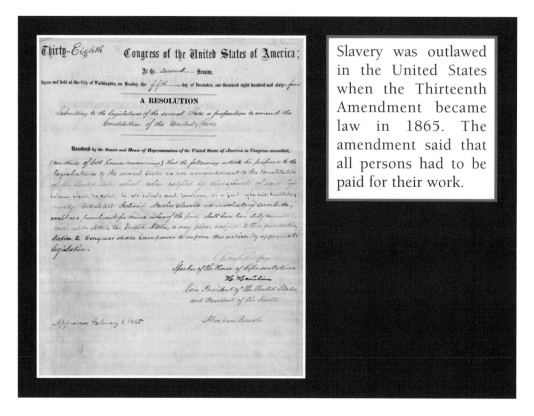

Slavery was outlawed in the United States when the Thirteenth Amendment became law in 1865. The amendment said that all persons had to be paid for their work.

Southern states. It ended in 1865. When the war ended, a new law was added to the United States Constitution. It guarantees the rights of all Americans. The new law made slavery illegal. It is known as the Thirteenth Amendment. The law meant that labor had to be provided by paid workers.

Political parties and politicians were always important in United States history. Politicians had the power to make and pass laws. Many politicians had wealthy friends.

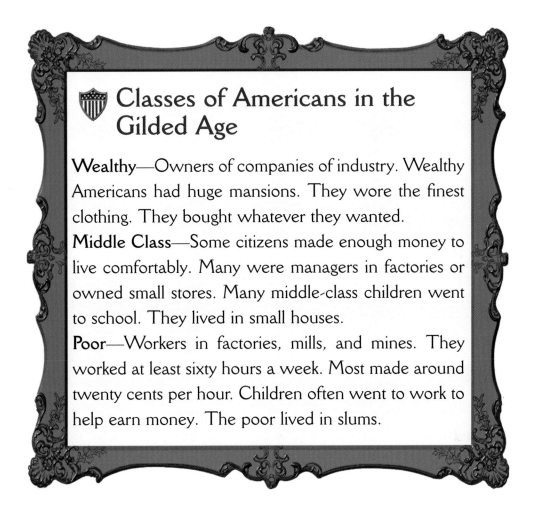

Classes of Americans in the Gilded Age

Wealthy—Owners of companies of industry. Wealthy Americans had huge mansions. They wore the finest clothing. They bought whatever they wanted.

Middle Class—Some citizens made enough money to live comfortably. Many were managers in factories or owned small stores. Many middle-class children went to school. They lived in small houses.

Poor—Workers in factories, mills, and mines. They worked at least sixty hours a week. Most made around twenty cents per hour. Children often went to work to help earn money. The poor lived in slums.

They included business owners. Soon the government was protecting the rights of wealthy Americans instead of all Americans.

Some political officials were dishonest. Businessmen offered money or bribes to the officials. Politicians

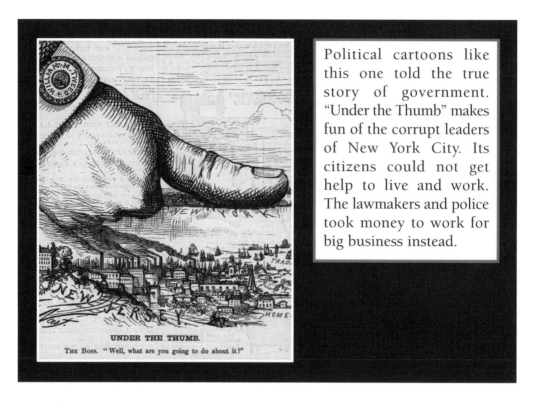

UNDER THE THUMB.

The Boss. "Well, what are you going to do about it?"

Political cartoons like this one told the true story of government. "Under the Thumb" makes fun of the corrupt leaders of New York City. Its citizens could not get help to live and work. The lawmakers and police took money to work for big business instead.

would then pass certain laws. The laws protected the businessmen. Police officers and judges also took bribes. They did not report or punish wealthy people who broke the law. Some political leaders also gave government jobs to supporters. Dishonest men were given important jobs in government. This brought more dishonesty into local, state, and national government.

The period after the Civil War is known as the Gilded Age. This name comes from a novel by Mark Twain and Charles Dudley Warner. The Gilded Age was a time of

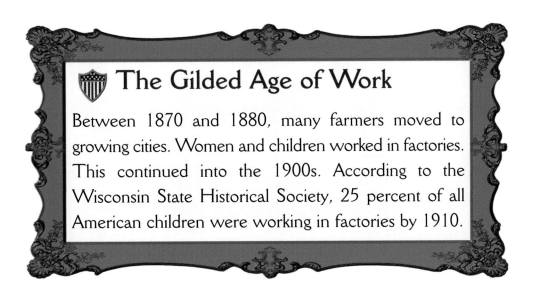

🛡 The Gilded Age of Work

Between 1870 and 1880, many farmers moved to growing cities. Women and children worked in factories. This continued into the 1900s. According to the Wisconsin State Historical Society, 25 percent of all American children were working in factories by 1910.

great wealth and horrible poverty. There were some very wealthy Americans. They included factory owners, officials, and bankers. There were also many poor Americans.

Many immigrants moved to growing cities to find work. The immigrants moved into run-down areas or slums. It was inexpensive to live in slums. Many immigrants did not have factory work experience. They had to do other jobs such as bricklaying or farm labor. These were very low-paying jobs. The slums continued to fill with immigrants and factory workers.

3

A Union to Save the Working Class

American industry helped many early towns grow. Resources such as fabrics and leather products were made and sold in large amounts. Small towns grew into large cities. Industrial factory owners became powerful. They did not have to treat their workers fairly. If a worker complained, he or she was fired. The jobs were often then given to immigrants. Immigrants were thankful for work. They worked for little pay and did not complain.

Small groups of workers began uniting to protect themselves. For example, the first labor union in Rochester, New Hampshire, was the Lasters' Protective Union. In 1884, the Wallace Company tried to pay workers less money. The union officials made a deal with the Wallace Company. The company did not cut wages. A

14

Peaceful strikes often became bloody when police showed up. City governments were on the side of the businesses. They quickly called out the police to break up the striking workers. Large unions worked through the violence. They often got a good settlement from companies.

few months later, union officials asked for a wage increase. The Wallace Company refused to pay more. The union ordered all its workers to strike. By striking, the union members stopped working for the company. The company agreed to increase wages after a two-week

strike. The company knew it could not make money without its workers. This was how early unions helped to change poor working conditions.

Unions began to organize wherever there were industries. Many unions were secret at first. Members did not tell anyone that they were in a union. Many companies fired workers who belonged to a union. Many employers would not hire someone in a union. This was called blacklisting. It was cheaper and easier to hire non-union workers.

Cities became crowded with laborers. Laborers made up the American working class. The working-class life of the Gilded Age was awful. A worker worked as many as sixteen hours each day. He or she lived in a slum and tenement housing. Disease was common because of unclean conditions. Crime was also common in the slums. Desperate people stole from one another. Everyone wanted to get out of the slums. Even five-year-old children worked in factories.

The poor watched as the wealthy lived well. The poor—skilled and unskilled laborers—knew that great wealth was possible. They also knew that it was unfair that others lived so well while they starved or got sick and died.

URIAH STEPHENS,
Founder of the K. of L.

Uriah Stephens helped form the Knights of Labor in 1869. The Knights of Labor wanted most to help the working class. Its members wanted to stop child labor. They demanded that fair wages be paid for all work.

The first national union to help the working class was the Noble and Holy Order of the Knights of Labor. It was also known as the Knights of Labor, or KOL. The KOL first formed in secret in 1869. Members talked about the union only at secret meetings. The union united skilled and unskilled laborers.

Uriah Stephens and five other members formed the KOL in Philadelphia, Pennsylvania. Stephens started it

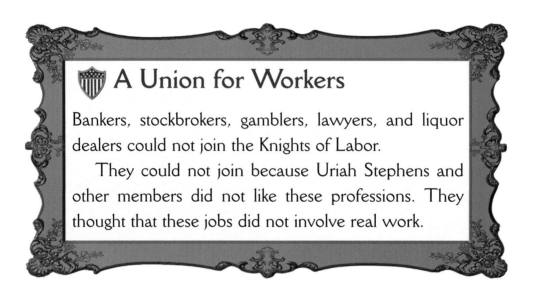

A Union for Workers

Bankers, stockbrokers, gamblers, lawyers, and liquor dealers could not join the Knights of Labor.

They could not join because Uriah Stephens and other members did not like these professions. They thought that these jobs did not involve real work.

during a local garment workers' meeting. Any worker who wanted to improve his life could join. Women workers were allowed to join the KOL in 1881.

4

The Knights of Labor

The Knights of Labor wanted to change working-class life. It wanted education for its children. It wanted better housing for its workers. It wanted members to enjoy the comforts of parks, libraries, and museums. The union wanted to elect honest people into government positions. These honest officials would fight against dishonest officials in the government. Only then would laws protecting workers be passed. The union also wanted industries to be owned and run by workers.

Union officials secretly taught workers about the labor movement. KOL officials secretly met with local unions such as Rochester's Lasters' Protective Union. Local unions were asked to join the KOL.

The main unit of the KOL was called the Home Chapter. It was based in New York. The Home Chapter

PREAMBLE

AND

DECLARATION OF PRINCIPLES

OF THE

KNIGHTS OF LABOR

OF AMERICA.

TO THE PUBLIC:

The alarming development and aggressiveness of great capitalists and corporations, unless checked, will inevitably lead to the pauperization and hopeless degradation of the toiling masses.

It is imperative, if we desire to enjoy the full blessings of life, that a check be placed upon unjust accumulation, and the power for evil of aggregated wealth.

This much-desired object can be accomplished only by the united efforts of those who obey the divine injunction, "In the sweat of thy face shalt thou eat bread."

Therefore we have formed the Order of Knights of Labor, for the purpose of organizing and directing the power of the industrial masses, not as a political party, for it is more—in it are crystallized sentiments and measures for the benefit of the whole people, but it should be borne in mind, when exercising the right of suffrage, that most of the objects herein set forth can only be obtained through legislation, and that it is the duty of all to assist in nominating and supporting with their votes only such candidates as will pledge their support to those measures, regardless of party. But no one shall, however, be compelled to vote with the majority, and calling upon all who believe in securing "the greatest good to the greatest number," to join and assist us, we declare to the world that our aims are:

I. To make industrial and moral worth, not wealth, the true standard of individual and National greatness.

II. To secure to the workers the full enjoyment of the wealth they create, sufficient leisure in which to develop their intellectual, moral and social faculties; all of the benefits, recreation and pleasures of association; in a word, to enable them to share in the gains and honors of advancing civilization.

In order to secure these results, we demand at the hands of the STATE:

III. The establishment of Bureaus of Labor Statistics, that we may arrive at a correct knowledge of the educational, moral and financial condition of the laboring masses.

IV. That the public lands, the heritage of the people, be reserved for actual settlers; not another acre for railroads or speculators, and that all lands now held for speculative purposes be taxed to their full value.

V. The abrogation of all laws that do not bear equally upon capital and labor, and the removal of unjust technicalities, delays and discriminations in the administration of justice.

VI. The adoption of measures providing for the health and safety of those engaged in mining and manufacturing, building industries, and for indemnification to those engaged therein for injuries received through lack of necessary safeguards.

VII. The recognition, by incorporation, of trades' unions, orders and such other associations as may be organized by the working masses to improve their condition and protect their rights.

VIII. The enactment of laws to compel corporations to pay their employees weekly, in lawful money, for the labor of the preceding week, and giving mechanics and laborers a first lien upon the product of their labor to the extent of their full wages.

IX. The abolition of the contract system on National, State and Municipal works.

X. The enactment of laws providing for arbitration between employers and employed, and to enforce the decision of the arbitrators.

XI. The prohibition by law of the employment of children under 15 years of age in workshops, mines and factories.

XII. To prohibit the hiring out of convict labor.

XIII. That a graduated income tax be levied.

And we demand at the hands of CONGRESS:

XIV. The establishment of a National monetary system, in which a circulating medium in necessary quantity shall issue direct to the people, without the intervention of banks; that all the National issue shall be full legal tender in payment of all debts, public and private; and that the Government shall not guarantee or recognize any private banks, or create any banking corporations.

XV. That interest-bearing bonds, bills of credit or notes shall never be issued by the Government, but that, when need arises, the emergency shall be met by issue of legal tender, non-interest-bearing money.

XVI. That the importation of foreign labor under contract be prohibited.

XVII. That, in connection with the post-office, the Government shall organize financial exchanges, safe deposits and facilities for deposit of the savings of the people in small sums.

XVIII. That the Government shall obtain possession, by purchase, under the right of eminent domain, of all telegraphs, telephones and railroads, and that hereafter no charter or license be issued to any corporation for construction or operation of any means of transporting intelligence, passengers or freight.

And while making the foregoing demands upon the State and National Government, we will endeavor to associate our own labors:

XIX. To establish co-operative institutions such as will tend to supersede the wage system, by the introduction of a co-operative industrial system.

XX. To secure for both sexes equal pay for equal work.

XXI. To shorten the hours of labor by a general refusal to work for more than eight hours.

XXII. To persuade employers to agree to arbitrate all differences which may arise between them and their employees, in order that the bonds of sympathy between them may be strengthened and that strikes may be rendered unnecessary.

If you believe in organization, you are earnestly invited to join with us in securing these objects. All information on the subject of organization should be sent to the General Secretary-Treasurer of the Order, who will have an Organizer visit you and assist in furthering the good work.

organized local chapters across the country. It showed unions how to bargain with employers. It taught unions how to strike if they could not get a bargain. The KOL organized strikes against railroad millionaire Jay Gould in 1885. News of the strikes spread across the country. Soon, thousands of people wanted to join the KOL.

KOL members elected a new leader in 1879. His name was Terence Powderly. Powderly came from an Irish immigrant family. He officially joined the Knights of Labor in 1876. He also became mayor of Scranton, Pennsylvania, in 1878.

KOL Goals:

- Shorter work hours—shifts cut down to eight hours
- Fewer weekly hours—sixty-hour workweeks cut down
- No child labor—child labor would be illegal
- Safer workplaces

The Knights of Labor printed a Declaration of Principles in 1885. The KOL did not want to strike against companies. It wanted to make deals with companies that helped workers. The KOL wanted to change working hours to just eight hours per day. Companies fought against the KOL. The KOL then held national strikes against large companies.

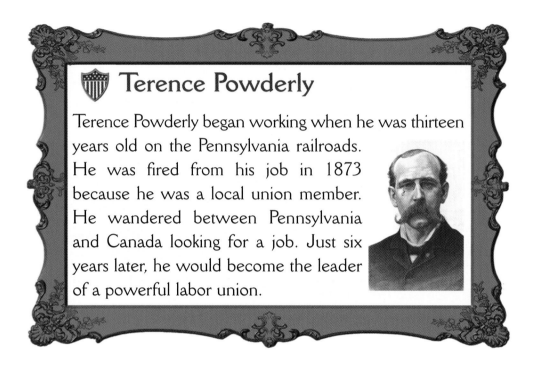

Terence Powderly

Terence Powderly began working when he was thirteen years old on the Pennsylvania railroads. He was fired from his job in 1873 because he was a local union member. He wandered between Pennsylvania and Canada looking for a job. Just six years later, he would become the leader of a powerful labor union.

Powderly served as the KOL leader from 1879 until 1893. He made the union public instead of secret. He organized the rules and goals of the national union. He told the union that he did not favor strikes. He wanted to bargain with employers rather than cause work to stop. The union had 80,000 members in 1885. There were 700,000 members within a year. Many workers joined because the union's power was growing.

5

The Haymarket Riot

During 1885 and 1886, union members focused on the goal of the eight-hour workday. The KOL and other union groups organized national strike days. Some Chicago union members wanted to overthrow the government. They were anarchists who wanted to fight.

Some police and factory-hired thugs often broke up union meetings and strikes in Chicago. Police captain John Bonfield led violent attacks against peaceful union gatherings. The thugs were known as Pinkertons. Pinkertons were private detectives from the Pinkerton Detective Agency. Founder Allen Pinkerton hired his detectives out to anyone needing their services.

The Knights of Labor planned a national strike for May 1, 1886. For months leading up to the strike, the Chicago anarchists printed and passed out papers. The papers called for action against police violence and unfair

RIOT AT McCORMICK'S REAPER WORKS,
Chicago, May 3, 1886.

The fighting that broke out at the McCormick Reaper Works in Chicago turned deadly. Shown on the left is a painting of the violence on that night in May 1886. The deaths of policemen turned the public against many unions. This hurt the KOL's chance to get the eight-hour workday for its members.

employers. Chicago citizens became worried that the strikes would be violent. About 300,000 strikers took part in the May 1 strike across the nation. About 40,000 members held strikes and meetings in Chicago. There was no violence on that day.

On May 3, anarchist August Spies held a meeting for nearly 3,000 Chicago strikers near the McCormick Reaper Works factory. Then the factory work whistle blew to start the day. The crowd Spies was talking to ran toward the factory. They were going to yell at people who worked even though there was a strike happening. The crowd threw stones at workers and the factory. Police stopped the violence by using clubs and guns against the strikers. One striker was killed.

A few anarchists such as Spies were upset that a union member was killed. They called for another meeting on May 4, 1886. The papers, or fliers, for the meeting said, "Attention Workingmen! Great mass meeting tonight at 7:30 at the Haymarket, Randolf Street . . . Workingmen arm yourselves and appear in Full Force!" Spies was asking the men to bring weapons and be ready to fight.

Over 3,000 people went to the Haymarket that night. Spies began speaking to the group at 8:30. The Chicago mayor, Carter Henry Harrison Jr., came to the meeting. He left after he made sure that the gathering was peaceful.

This anarchist flyer is printed in both English and German. Many of the workers at the Chicago reaper works were German immigrants. August Spies used many of these poor immigrants to start the fighting. The Haymarket Riot gave unions and German immigrants a bad name for many years.

Captain Bonfield and 180 police officers then ordered the crowd to go away. Someone from the crowd threw a bomb at the police. It killed seven officers and wounded about sixty others.

The person who threw the bomb was never found. Newspapers favored the police, saying that union anarchists caused the death of noble officers. The deaths gave unions a bad name. People began to think that unions meant violence. Eight anarchist members were charged with the murders. They were charged because

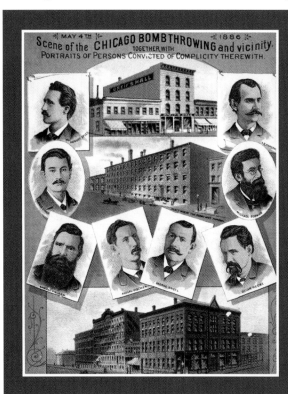

The convicted murderers of the Haymarket Riot are (*from left to right*): August Spies, Louis Lingg, Samuel Fielden, Adolph Fischer, George Engel, Oscar Neebe, Michael Schwab, and Albert Parsons.

they had spoken publicly against the police. This included August Spies.

The eight union workers were found guilty of murder by the Cook County Court of Illinois. The eight appealed, or tried to get the Supreme Court to change the court's decision. The appeals did not work. On November 11, 1887, four of the members were hanged.

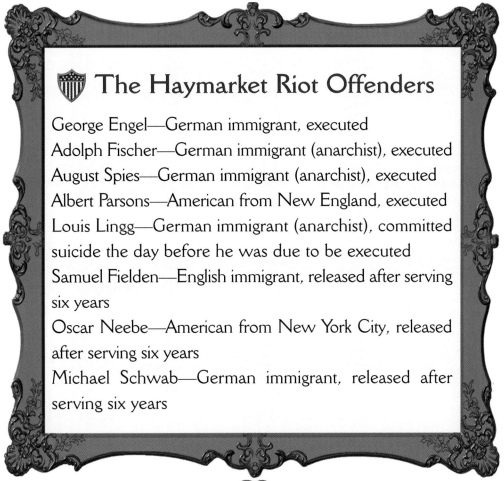

The Haymarket Riot Offenders

George Engel—German immigrant, executed

Adolph Fischer—German immigrant (anarchist), executed

August Spies—German immigrant (anarchist), executed

Albert Parsons—American from New England, executed

Louis Lingg—German immigrant (anarchist), committed suicide the day before he was due to be executed

Samuel Fielden—English immigrant, released after serving six years

Oscar Neebe—American from New York City, released after serving six years

Michael Schwab—German immigrant, released after serving six years

A day before the hanging, one of the eight killed himself in prison. Six years later, three remaining members were set free. They were set free because there was not enough evidence to tie them to the bombing.

The Haymarket Riot was the beginning of the end for the KOL. Powderly tried to separate the union from the murderers. He said that the eight were bad representatives of any union effort. Much of the American public, however, would not forget that murders happened from union activities. Powderly left the KOL in 1893. By 1900, the union had lost the favor of workers and nearly disappeared. Many unions stopped fighting for the eight-hour workday. Workers finally gained the eight-hour workday after laws were passed in 1933.

Many people in Chicago felt that the rioters were wrongly convicted. They wore brass lapel pins to show their anger. The pin (*above*) shows a hangman's gallows and noose.

Glossary

anarchist (**AN-ar-kist**)   A person who believes in no order and no control.

bargain (**BAR-guhn**)   To discuss until a deal is made.

blacklisting (**BLAK-lis-ting**)   Keeping someone from work because of union membership.

bribe (**BRYB**)   Money or gift offered to get someone to do something.

employee (**im-PLOY-ee**)   A person who works for and is paid by a business.

Gilded Age (**GIL-duhd AJE**)   The period of time after the Civil War.

illegal (**il-LEE-guhl**)   Against the law.

industry (**IN-duh-stree**)   A business or trade.

labor laws (**LAY-bur LAWZ**)   Laws that made certain business practices illegal.

labor movement (**LAY-bur MOOV-muhnt**)   A group of people joined in the belief that labor conditions could be improved.

represent (**reh-prih-ZENT**)   To speak or act for someone else.

shift (**SHIFT**)   A set period of hours of work.

strike (**STRYK**)   To refuse to work in order to get better working conditions.

union (**YOON-yun**)   An organized group of workers set up to improve working conditions.

workload (**WURK-lohd**)   The amount of work a worker is expected to do.

Web Sites

Due to the changing nature of Internet links, the Rosen Publishing Group, Inc., has developed an online list of Web sites related to the subject of this book. This site is updated regularly. Please use this link to access the list:

http://www.rosenlinks.com/aistc/klhr

Primary Source Image List

Page 5: 1873 engraving "Little Laborers of New York City" in *Harper's New Monthly Magazine*. Housed at the Library of Congress, Washington, D.C.

Page 6: Photograph of 1851 membership card, Amalgamated Society of Engineers.

Page 7: Nineteenth-century photograph of labor union leader Samuel Gompers.

Page 10: Transcript of the Thirteenth Amendment to the U.S. Constitution (abolishing slavery). Housed at the National Archives, Washington, D.C.

Page 12: "Under the Thumb" illustration in *Harper's Weekly*, 1871.

Page 15: Illustration of streetcar operator's strike, by T. de Thulstrup, in *Harper's Weekly*, 1886.

Page 17: Circa 1865 engraving of Uriah Smith Stephens, fellow founder of the Knights of Labor.

Page 20: Preamble and Declaration of Principles of the Knights of Labor, circa 1885. Housed at the Chicago Historical Society, Chicago, Illinois.

Page 22: 1886 wood engraving of Terence Vincent Powderly. Housed at the Library of Congress, Washington, D.C.

Page 24: 1887 painting by Paul J. Morand of men fighting at the McCormick Reaper Works. Housed at the Chicago Historical Society, Chicago, Illinois.

Page 25: 1886 handbill circulated by August Spies. Housed at the Chicago Historical Society, Chicago, Illinois.

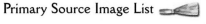

Index

About the Author

Bernadette Brexel is a journalist and photographer from Omaha, Nebraska. She attended the University of Nebraska and Parsons in Paris.